Living in Space

Sharon Dalgleish

sundance™

A Haights Cross Communications Company

sundance™

A Haights Cross Communications ◀ Company

Copyright © 2003 Sundance Publishing

Published by
Sundance Publishing
P.O. Box 1326
234 Taylor Street
Littleton, MA 01460
800-343-8204
www.sundancepub.com

Copyright © text Sharon Dalgleish
Copyright © illustrations Matt Lin and Cliff Watt

First published 2002 by
Blake Education, Locked Bag 2022, Glebe 2037, Australia
Exclusive United States Distribution: Sundance Publishing

Design by Cliff Watt in association with
Sundance Publishing

Living in Space
ISBN 0-7608-6695-3

Photo Credits:
pp. 6–8 NASA; p. 9 (top) NASA, (center) photolibrary.com, (bottom) NASA;
p. 11 (top and center) NASA, (bottom left) APL/Corbis, (bottom right) NASA;
p. 14 (top) NASA; p. 15 photolibrary.com; pp. 16–18 NASA;
p. 19 (top) photolibrary.com, (bottom) NASA; pp. 20–21 NASA;
pp. 24–25 NASA; p. 26 Space Island Group; p. 28–29 NASA.

Printed in Canada

Table of Contents

The Race to Space

Would you like to travel through space at 29.8 kilometers per second (18.5 miles/sec)? Too bad if your answer is no . . . because that's just what you are doing right now!

You are hurtling through space at this speed as Earth orbits the sun. Your spaceship is planet Earth. It keeps your life support system—air, water, energy, and livable temperature—intact. But can you leave Earth and explore the rest of space?
Look up at the moon in the night sky. What would it be like to leave our planet and actually go there? It isn't easy to break free from Earth's **atmosphere.** But in the twentieth century, people developed the technical ability to do just that!

Getting There

You don't float away from Earth because Earth's gravity pulls you down to the ground. Space travel is only possible if you can escape the massive pull of gravity.

Around 1500, Chinese scientist Wan Hoo tried to fly. He used 47 rockets tied to his chair. The rockets blasted off, and Wan Hoo was never seen again!

Escape Velocity

To escape Earth's gravity, you need to travel at the incredible speed of 11 kilometers per second (7 miles/sec). Any slower, and you will fall back to the ground. The only thing powerful enough to reach that speed is a rocket. As far back as 1150, the Chinese used rockets powered by gunpowder to launch flaming arrows at their enemies. It wasn't until 1903 that a Russian scientist proposed the idea that rockets could use liquid fuel to overcome gravity. Many scientists then worked on developing his idea as a way to reach space.

HOW ATTRACTIVE ARE YOU?

In 1666, Isaac Newton saw an apple fall in his garden. He wondered why the apple fell toward the ground and not away from it. He thought an attractive force must be acting on the apple. He called it "gravity." Newton said that the strength of gravitational attraction between two objects relies on two factors. One is the distance between the objects. The other is the mass, or amount of matter, in the objects. So you're not very "attractive" compared to something as big as Earth!

American Robert Goddard (1882–1945) was the first person to use liquid fuel to fire a rocket, in 1926. The press made fun of Goddard because he talked about a rocket one day reaching the moon.

It Takes More Than One

After World War II, rocket research really took off. But the first rockets didn't have the power to completely escape gravity, and they could only reach low orbit. The solution was to build rockets that work in stages. As each stage uses up its fuel, it drops away. This makes the rocket lighter, so it can travel faster and faster until it escapes into space.

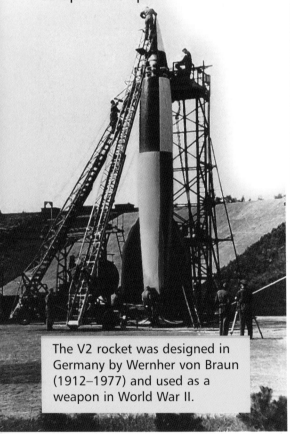

The V2 rocket was designed in Germany by Wernher von Braun (1912–1977) and used as a weapon in World War II.

THE SATURN V

After the war, von Braun went to America where he helped design the biggest rocket ever built—the Saturn V.

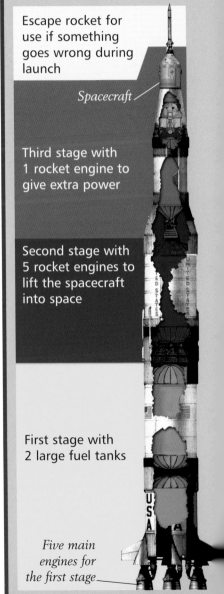

Escape rocket for use if something goes wrong during launch

Spacecraft

Third stage with 1 rocket engine to give extra power

Second stage with 5 rocket engines to lift the spacecraft into space

First stage with 2 large fuel tanks

Five main engines for the first stage

Survival Tests

Once people knew that rockets could reach space, the race was on to get humans out there.

Sputnik 1 carried a small radio that sent "bleeping" signals for 21 days as it orbited the Earth.

Animal Astronauts

Before scientists dared send a human into space, they needed information about whether a living thing could survive there. In 1957, the Soviet Union launched *Sputnik 1* to see if they could get an artificial **satellite** into orbit. When that succeeded, they sent the first living Earth creature into space—a dog named Laika. But there was no way to return the satellite to Earth, and Laika died in space. Then in 1959, two American monkeys, Able and Baker, became the first creatures to be sent into space and brought home again.

Laika is shown on board *Sputnik 2* in 1957. Instruments sent data back to Earth about her pulse and heartbeat. She died a week after launch when her oxygen supply ran out.

Monkey Able is strapped in before being launched into space in the nose cone of a *Jupiter* missile. Able died as a result of the mission, but Baker lived until 1984.

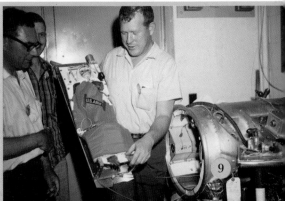

People Pioneers

On April 12, 1961, the Soviet Union succeeded in getting the first human being into space. Yuri Gagarin made a single orbit of Earth inside a tiny spacecraft, *Vostok 1*. The next month, Alan Shepard became the first American in space when he went on a 15-minute mission into space. In 1969, the U.S. *Apollo 11* astronauts walked on the moon and flew safely home. Since then, space missions and exploration have continued.

Life on board early spacecraft was not very comfortable. Inside the **capsule,** there was sitting room only, with the crew forced to wear bulky space suits. And astronauts in space can get travel sickness—just like you might in a car. But you don't want to throw up in space. It floats around in globules and can damage equipment!

Yuri Gagarin's orbit lasted about 89 minutes. To return to Earth, he ejected from the spacecraft and used a parachute to fall the last 4 km (2 ½ miles)!

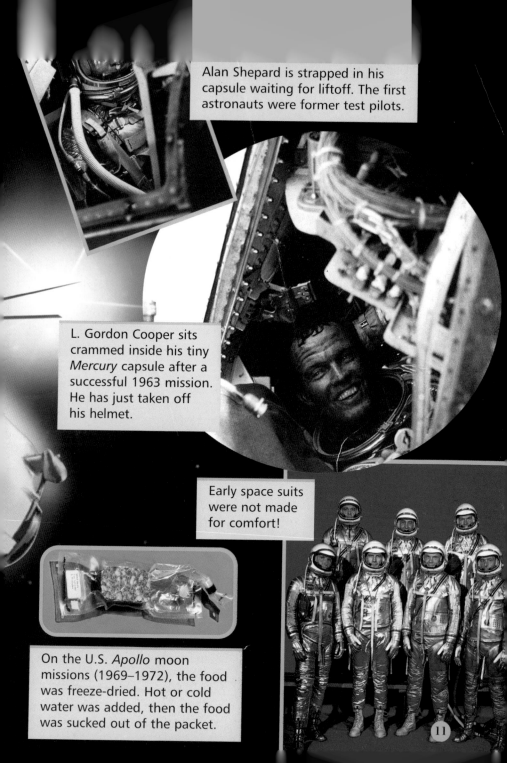

Alan Shepard is strapped in his capsule waiting for liftoff. The first astronauts were former test pilots.

L. Gordon Cooper sits crammed inside his tiny *Mercury* capsule after a successful 1963 mission. He has just taken off his helmet.

Early space suits were not made for comfort!

On the U.S. *Apollo* moon missions (1969–1972), the food was freeze-dried. Hot or cold water was added, then the food was sucked out of the packet.

It's a Job

**Help wanted! Must not go crazy
when trapped in small places.
Must be able to work upside down.
Have you got what it takes?
Then apply for the next shuttle mission!**

We've come a long way since our early quick trips
into space. The biggest advance came with the
space shuttle. It launches like a rocket, but lands
on a runway like an airplane. And best of all—it's
reusable, which means it's a lot less expensive than
the old one-shot rockets. This shuttle **orbiter** is
launched on the back of a giant fuel tank plus two
large rocket boosters. The fuel tank and boosters
drop away after a successful launch. People then
live and work inside the orbiter as it circles
Earth, until the crew lands it safely back home.

So . . . are you ready for your first mission?
10, 9, 8, 7, 6, 5, 4, 3, 2, 1—blast off!

Dinner is prepared in the galley on a space shuttle mission.

Life in Free Fall

Away from Earth's gravity, even everyday tasks can be tricky.

Crumbs!

Don't Play with Your Food

You're over the worst of your travel sickness. Now you're ready to eat a tasty dinner. In the early days of space travel, dinner was a paste sucked out of tubes like toothpaste. On the shuttle, the food looks a little more like real food! Take a look at the **galley,** or kitchen. You'll see

WHAT A CHOICE!

Today, astronauts have about 100 choices of food and 50 choices of drink. They even get to try out the products and choose menus before the mission.

Dinner Menu Day 1

Shrimp cocktail

Beef steak

Macaroni and cheese

Strawberry drink

Tea

Note: We cannot serve crumbly foods. The crumbs would float around like a dust storm.

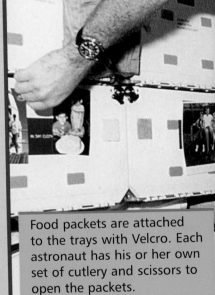

Food packets are attached to the trays with Velcro. Each astronaut has his or her own set of cutlery and scissors to open the packets.

that many foods are **dehydrated** and in plastic pouches. Add water to the pouch, then squish it around. Your food is now ready to eat! Be careful that your dinner doesn't float away, though. Uncover only a little at a time as you eat it. Sticky foods are the easiest. Don't forget to grab a drink bag with a straw. You'll need to suck through a straw even if it's a hot drink. Liquid doesn't pour in space!

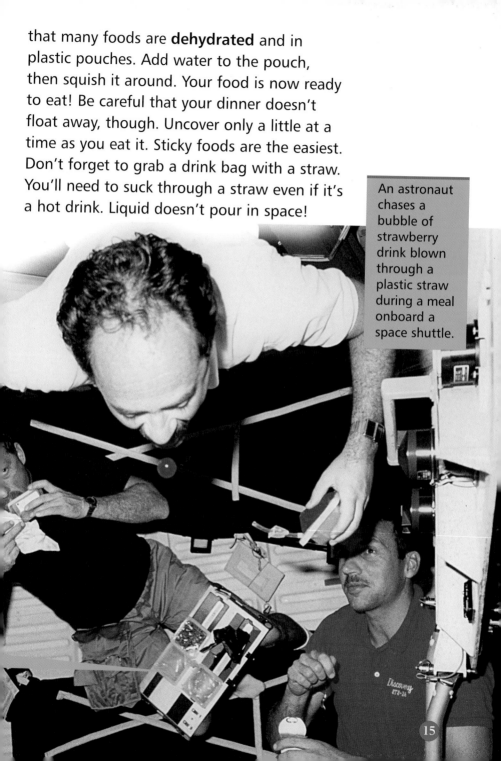

An astronaut chases a bubble of strawberry drink blown through a plastic straw during a meal onboard a space shuttle.

15

Work Those Muscles

Don't forget to get some exercise before bed. On Earth, the lower body and legs carry the weight of the body. Floating around in space means you aren't using the muscles in that part of your body, and so they weaken. Even your bones can weaken—so hop on that treadmill now.

Keeping Clean

You won't be able to take a shower after your workout. There isn't one on the shuttle. You'll have to take a sponge bath. You can clean your teeth, though. Just make sure you swallow the

Treadmill exercise is a key part of space shuttle missions.

 WHAT WILL YOUR PHOTOS LOOK LIKE?

Changes in gravity have some strange effects on the human body, so your friends may not recognize you in your space photos. On Earth, the fluids inside your body are held down by gravity. In space, they are not held down at all. They spread throughout your body, right up to your head. That's why some astronauts talk about having a moon face. Your space face will look puffy and fat, but your legs will look skinny like chicken legs! And the bones in your spine will float apart, so you will be 2.5–5 cm (1–2 in.) taller!

toothpaste or spit it in a towel. Otherwise it will be floating around until you get back to Earth! Going to the bathroom is an adventure. First, you strap yourself onto the toilet and attach the suction hose. And so that whatever you leave behind in the toilet doesn't float out, a fan pushes the waste away. Then it is dehydrated and stored until the return to Earth.

Special rinse-free shampoo is used on a space shuttle mission.

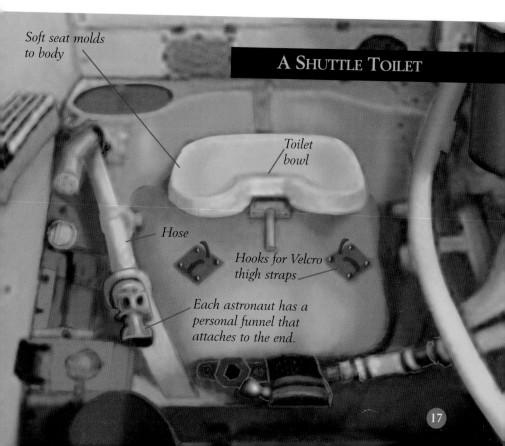

Soft seat molds to body

A SHUTTLE TOILET

Toilet bowl

Hose

Hooks for Velcro thigh straps

Each astronaut has a personal funnel that attaches to the end.

ZZZZZZZZZZ

It's time for bed. To prevent bouncing off the walls in your sleep, first zip yourself into a sleeping bag. Then attach yourself to a wall, seat, or bunk. The sun rises and sets every 45 minutes as you **orbit** Earth. So, if you want to sleep in the **cockpit,** you'll need an eye mask. On the other hand, you can't complain about a lumpy mattress!

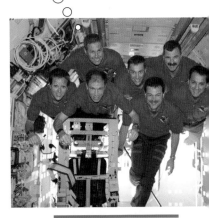

Now I can drift off to sleep.

A change of shift occurs onboard a space shuttle.

Sleeping on a space shuttle is quite a change from sleeping on Earth. But there is a little pillow you can fasten to your head with a strap!

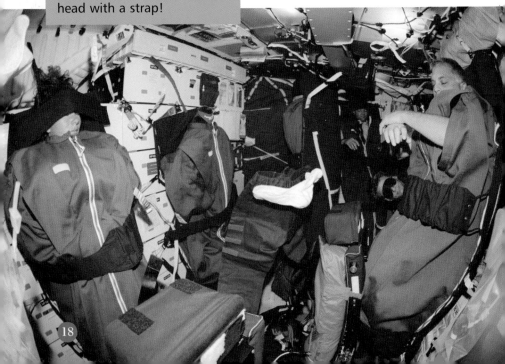

Jobs in Space

Crew wake-up call! Flight day 2 and there's work to be done!

Who Does What?

Your mission flight plan sets out work for each day on board. You could be the commander in charge of the spacecraft, the pilot, or a mission specialist trained to do a specific job for this mission. If you have one of these jobs, you are an astronaut. Or you could be a **payload specialist.** These are the scientists, doctors, or engineers who do experiments in space. Your mission will last up to two and a half weeks—with no weekends off!

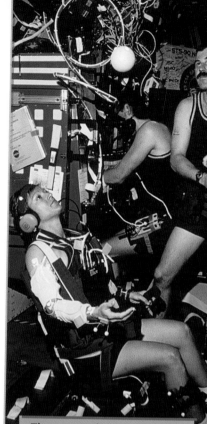

These people on a space shuttle mission are testing how the human body adapts to low gravity conditions in space.

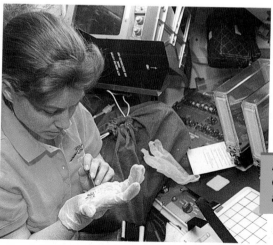

An experiment is being done with a tiny plant on a space shuttle.

Stepping Out

One of the most daring jobs on a mission involves going outside the shuttle. This could be to capture and repair a satellite, to test new equipment, or to work on the International Space Station. If this is your job, you'll need to wear a complicated space suit—unless you want a quick and painful death! You'll feel a bit like a robot because you can only make very small, slow movements. Be thankful for that thick, heavy suit, though. It's all there is between you and tiny bits of space dust that are as dangerous as bullets. It also protects you from hot and cold temperatures and the airless **vacuum** of space. So if you get a hole in your space suit, you'll be in a lot of trouble!

This astronaut is on a space walk to repair the Hubble Space Telescope.

 DO I HAVE TO WEAR THE SUIT?

If you jumped out of a submarine at the bottom of the ocean, the pressure of the water would crush you. In space, the opposite happens. Space is a vacuum—there is no atmosphere. Where there is no atmosphere, any **molecules** in the area want to spread out as much as possible. So, if you stepped out of the shuttle without wearing a special space suit, your molecules would spread out. Then you would blow up like a big balloon—until you finally popped.

THE PROTECTIVE SPACE SUIT

This space suit is like a mini-Earth, providing everything a human needs for life—but only for seven hours.

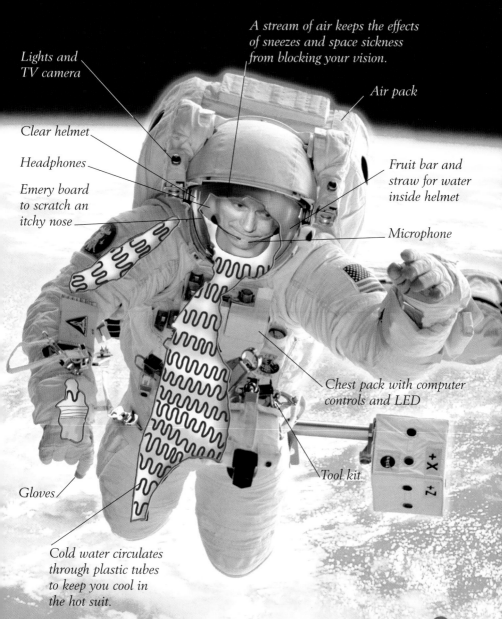

A stream of air keeps the effects of sneezes and space sickness from blocking your vision.

Lights and TV camera

Air pack

Clear helmet

Headphones

Fruit bar and straw for water inside helmet

Emery board to scratch an itchy nose

Microphone

Chest pack with computer controls and LED

Tool kit

Gloves

Cold water circulates through plastic tubes to keep you cool in the hot suit.

Space Stations and Beyond

**Space for rent! Ever-changing view!
Best space sports facilities in the universe!
Only $60,000,000,000.00! Don't miss out!
Blast off for an inspection today.**

Some day in the future you might read an ad like
this one. **Space stations** have been hanging around
above Earth since Salyut 1 was launched by the
Soviet Union in 1971. The latest is the International
Space Station (ISS). Unlike a space shuttle, the ISS is
designed to be in permanent orbit. Astronauts and
scientists are transported by shuttle to and from the
station. They can live there for months, or even a
year, and carry out experiments and research.
Doctors continue to study how well human bodies
cope with living in space for these longer periods of
time. Then, who knows what will be next? Space
hotels? Space cities? A colony on the moon?

The ISS Is Coming!

What's 73m (240 ft) wide and weighs more than a million pounds? It's not an oversized construction toy—it's the International Space Station (ISS)!

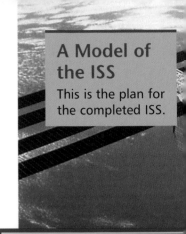

A Model of the ISS

This is the plan for the completed ISS.

Floating Construction Zone

In 1998, two astronauts on a space walk connected the first two parts of the ISS. The station is an international effort, with 16 countries working together to build it. These include the United States, Russia, Canada, Japan, Brazil, and 11 member countries of the European Space Agency.

It's Just the Beginning

The ISS will be a testing ground for future plans. Space stations could be used as factories for manufacturing new types of materials and medicines. Without gravity, some medical operations might be easier and safer to perform there. Space stations could also be used to launch missions into deep space. Because the station is already free from Earth's gravity, spacecraft launched from it could be much bigger and wouldn't need as much fuel to get going.

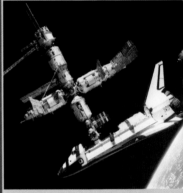

RECORD BREAKER

The *Mir* space station smashed every record in the book, including longest stay in space. It was launched by the Soviet Union in 1986 and was crewed until 1999. It paved the way for the ISS. This photo shows space shuttle *Atlantis* joined to *Mir* by a special docking adapter.

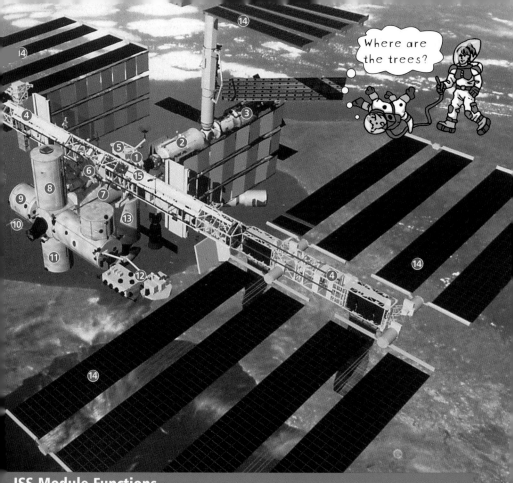

ISS Module Functions

1. Connects other modules
2. Provides power and propulsion
3. Current station's living quarters
4. "Backbone" of the stations, supports the modules
5. A way in and out for space walks
6. Robotic arm to help build station
7. Science lab
8. Effects of gravity studied here
9. Science lab
10. Links other modules to station
11. Lab with platform for experiments in space
12. Returns crew to Earth in an emergency
13. Living quarters
14. Solar panels to produce power
15. Observation port

The Space Island Group has plans for a ring-shaped, rotating hotel built out of 12 empty NASA shuttle fuel tanks. The inside would be divided into two or three decks, with cabins similar to those on a cruise ship.

Beyond Station Life

It's not science fiction . . . space tourism is already here. And NASA has futuristic plans for colonies of humans on Mars and the moon.

Space Tourists.

Book Your Tickets Now!

One day, taking a spaceship to a vacation destination might be as common as taking an airplane is today. The first paying space tourist was a sixty-year-old American, Dennis Tito. He paid the Russian Space Agency about $20 million to take him to the ISS in 2001. His space holiday lasted eight days. While he was there, he helped prepare food for the astronauts. Some holiday! The ISS isn't the only vacation destination. A private company called the Space Island Group has big plans to build a space hotel. The whole hotel would rotate once per minute, creating a gravitational pull one-third as strong as Earth's. But don't expect great views; there are no plans for windows. The rotation speed would be so fast that tourists would get sick if they looked out.

In space sports facilities, a whole new range of activities will be possible.

From the Moon to Mars

NASA has been developing plans for a colony on the moon since the 1970s. Don't expect one any time soon, though. A moon colony would probably cost trillions of dollars. In 1998, frozen water was discovered at the poles of the moon. If water *is* available on the moon, it solves many problems. It could be used for drinking and for growing plants to eat. It could also be converted to oxygen for breathing and to hydrogen for rocket fuel.

This drawing shows a possible mining base on the moon. One idea is to use raw material mined on the moon for a lunar metals production plant.

This drawing shows where workers on the moon might live.

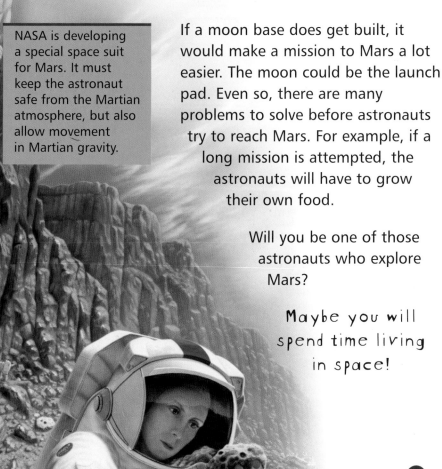

NASA is developing a special space suit for Mars. It must keep the astronaut safe from the Martian atmosphere, but also allow movement in Martian gravity.

If a moon base does get built, it would make a mission to Mars a lot easier. The moon could be the launch pad. Even so, there are many problems to solve before astronauts try to reach Mars. For example, if a long mission is attempted, the astronauts will have to grow their own food.

Will you be one of those astronauts who explore Mars?

Maybe you will spend time living in space!

Fact File

Living in space is changing life on Earth. Here are just a few of the space technologies now used on Earth.

TECHNOLOGY

1. gel inserts in shoes
2. plastic diapers
3. battery-powered tools
4. small pumps
5. infrared cameras
6. bar codes
7. type of ultrasound
8. toxic vapor detector

USE IN SPACE

1. helped Apollo astronauts to walk on rocky surface of Moon
2. a way to deal with human waste in early, cramped space capsules
3. used to drill into surface of moon to collect samples
4. used in space shuttle fuel pumps
5. to check blazing plumes from a space shuttle
6. to keep track of spacecraft parts
7. to detect microscopic flaws in spacecraft
8. to detect carbon monoxide on *Skylab*

SPIN-OFF USE ON EARTH

1. in sports shoes to make them comfortable
2. disposable diapers for babies
3. cordless power tools
4. small pumps in artificial human heart
5. firefighters use to scan fires for hot spots
6. pricing in supermarkets
7. to assess skin damage in burn victims
8. smoke detectors in houses

Glossary

atmosphere the mixture of gases surrounding Earth, or any other planet or star

capsule a small spacecraft with just enough room inside for the crew to fit

cockpit the area where the pilot sits

dehydrated something that has had the moisture taken out of it

galley the kitchen of a ship, airplane, or spacecraft

molecules the smallest particles of a substance able to exist on their own

orbit the path of a satellite around a planet, or a planet around the Sun

orbiter the part of the space shuttle that is like an airplane

payload specialist professionals who do experiments in space

satellite an object in orbit; for example, a moon is a natural satellite, but a spacecraft is an artificial satellite

space shuttle a reusable spacecraft that carries people and cargo into orbit

space station a large, crewed spacecraft that stays in space for several years

vacuum airless space, empty of all matter

space station

Index